Why Did They Kill Me?
by

Ebelver Brown Lewis

DEDICATION

A special thank you to my sons Anthony and Vincent for their unconditional love and support. To my brothers Eddie and Hosea for their solid strength and advice. To my sisters Etta and Eartha for always having a listening ear , and my cousin Appolonia for nursing me back to health. To my dear friends Carolyn, Leah and Mark for being my friends when I was difficult to befriend. Last but not least, to my friend Renita Smith for not only contributing to this book, but for also pushing me to complete the work.

Thank you and I sincerely love you all!

Acknowledgements

Renita Smith is an educator, author and poet. She has over 30 years' experience in education and is the author of such works as *"Somebody Needs to Hear What I Have to Say,"* *"Reflections of My Inner Self: Contemporary Writings for Self-Empowerment"*, and editor of *"A No Fail Approach to the Writing Process"*. She brilliantly captures the hearts of feelings of many others through her poetry and written works. Ms. Smith is the creator of the poems you will experience in this writing. You will want to collect all of her work after you feel and connect with her expressions.

Table of Contents

Why Did They Kill Me?

Foreword:

"WHY DID THEY KILL ME?"

For my loved ones who have passed on and those who have decided to rise and live again.

I remember very vividly seeing my uncle for the last time in the hospital. He was 29 years old and had 26 or so bullet holes in his body. He had suffered so many wounds and speculation was rapid that the shots were intended for someone else. How tragic. The last thing I remember him asking was "Why did they kill me?" Immediately after the question was posed to my mother, I passed out. The thought of someone being riddled with bullets and consciously feeling this was a mistake, just overtook me.

When I began writing my thoughts and seeking to live a fulfilled and joyful life, I recognized that so much of my optimism and excitement about the possibilities in life were no longer present. My ambition and hopefulness were no longer present.

I searched to find out why these things were now missing. I discovered that the answers were somehow intertwined with my interactions and relationships with people. Some shot me down with words, cut me with a look, while others stabbed me with betrayal. I had also shortened my own life by internalizing things that had nothing to do with me. The result was still the same. I felt my true spirit had been murdered and I had been left with an empty void. Not only did I want to know why I **allowed** others to **kill** who I was, but also needed to know how to be revived so that I can be happy and fulfilled again. I hope these memoirs and poems help others along this journey as well.

Question #1 Am I Dead?

It was a Saturday morning and I sat at my breakfast table with my coffee AND my bible. I was there alone, which was my condition ninety-five percent of the time for the past 10 years or so. I realized that my connection to God was not what I felt it should be, nor was it what it had been in the distant past. I wanted so desperately to reconnect, but did not know quite where or how to start. I began to pray for direction and guidance as to which scripture I should read. This attempt at meditation and reconnection was different from so many of my previous attempts. This attempt to reach out to God felt more like a life or death situation. I started praying and "reading" the bible so many times before!

Well, let's look at how it had even begun. I had gotten up and gone to the bathroom to begin my normal morning routine. I looked into the mirror and it felt as if a stranger was looking back at me. "Who are you?" "What happened to me?" "Is she (**me**) gone for good?" I bowed my head and began to pray.

I don't remember if I felt more lost, broken or just frightened!

Sitting at the table, I said "Lord, I need you to help me...PLEASE! Help me find myself." I turned a couple of pages and stopped at Luke 24. I hesitated and thought, "Uhmm, Easter was last week." But, instead of moving on, I begin to read. When I reached verse 5, it read, "And as they were afraid, and bowed down their faces to the earth, they said unto them why seek ye the living among the dead?" Just as the news hit when you realize you've lost a loved one, I began to weep uncontrollably. I realized that yes, she (me) had died!! I cried out, "Lord, am I dead!" That went on for several minutes. I was extremely distraught because I realized the answer was "YES." Ask yourself, are you dead?

I recognized that although I had been walking, talking, breathing and moving, I was no longer among the living. I was truly only going through the motions. The person I was had died several years ago. So, as with any other death, my next question was, "How did she die?" No cancer, no accident, no illness. She was young and strong. What had taken out this once happy and youthful life? My doctor had already verified that I had no signs of heart failure. But oh, I think **THAT'S it.**

I began to look back at all the murdered dreams, the cancerous relationships and the dark bruises from one disappointment after another. I couldn't leave out the time my heart was attacked, and I was left to suffer slowly and painfully alone. The stabbings from so called friends and emotional aneurysms from trying to understand complicated family dynamics and interactions. Yes, she (I) had been murdered even by self-inflicted cuts and wounds brought on by guilt and shame.

I continued reading to verse 11 and it says, "the words seemed as idle tales." Just as my own true story if told, some would choose not to believe all those tales of abuse, back stabbings, and narrow escapes and the witnessing of violence forced on loved ones. Some were the stories that movies are made of. But I continued reading and was determined to not be discouraged In verse 17 He asked me "Why am I sad." My reply was simply because of all these negative emotions, encounters and experiences that I eluted to previously. Reading on, I understood that there was a different reference in verse 26 when it talks about the things Christ had suffered. But for my purposes (and I believe that's how God answers), it was a reminder that yes, Christ had suffered ALL for me. I tried in vain to remember a promise He made to me and had failed to keep. Instead, I remembered that HE had bore all the same pains and disappointments. Why am I bearing them all over again? Why am I CHOOSING to die over and over again?

Verse 31." And their eyes were opened, and they knew him, and He vanished out of their sight." I sat a while longer, just mediating on His suffering and His promises. This brought back to my remembrance how he has not failed to fulfill any of His promises to me. So again, I asked, "Lord am I dead?" this time the answer was "NO!" He is risen in me because He has already bore all my pain, all my burdens and all my suffering or disappointments. I chose to go and live again. I chose not to lay down and die.

I went back to the bathroom and cleaned myself up. I praised and gave thanks to God, for I knew I did not have to be among the walking dead. I no longer had to live anxiously or worried. I am not called to give up, but to live in abundance and to live free.

I thank God for his word and the revelation of its power.

Am I Dead?

As I sit here
So, all alone
My connection to God
Is almost gone

I need you Lord
To rescue me
Take me back
Where I need to be

As I pause
And pray to you
For complete direction
In what I should do

A look in the mirror
A reflection of me
God Am I dead?
How could this be

Pain and disappointments
Have consumed my soul
Praying to you Lord
Again, to be whole

A message from God
Then appeared to me
Don't fret my child
You are yet free

I have already
Paid the price
You Are Not Dead
My grace will suffice

~Renita L. Smith

Reflections

Question #2   Is Ignorance Bliss or Just Blindness?

When I look back over my life, I am somewhat astonished at how truly "ignorant" (or not knowing), I was about so many things. I spent so many years as a babe in Christ as well as a babe in life. I was one of those foolish people who had just enough knowledge to be dangerous to themselves. I lacked the wisdom and understanding needed to apply any knowledge in a meaningful and fruitful way. I was not a bad or evil person, but I was certainly an ignorant one (again, not knowing)

My ex-spouse constantly made reference to the idiom, "Ignorance is bliss." I didn't know it at the time, but I assume now that he was referring to my apparent "happy" marriage during his extensive years of having an affair. I had no knowledge or understanding of how our lives were being shaped by the things I was blinded to. I had no understanding of how spoken words would cause chaos and irreconcilable destruction in both our lives. I was laughing at things while not knowing that I was the joke of it all. The bible warns against jesting and clowning around. After diving deeper into God's word, I now cringe when I hear couples speak negative things on their spouses, even in the name of joking or clowning around.

It's amazing how people spend so much time trying to live a righteous or more spiritual life, only to be defiled by their own words. According to Mark 7:15, the thing that defiles a man is not what goes into his mouth, but what comes out of his mouth. I had to learn the hard way that sometimes wisdom can be imparted or passed down, but other times its gained through trials.

I was molded from a young age to be obedient and to not be free willed. This stifled me in many ways and I often found myself frustrated and angry. I didn't know (ignorant to the knowledge) how to project my interest or talents without being told I was selfish or self-centered. This caused me to just become angry and self-conscious about everything I did. I found myself being lost and locked into always trying to make others feel comfortable with what I wanted or needed. I tried to be whatever I felt others expected of me. Out of ignorance, I learned to become "more" or "less" to appease others. But the worse thing I learned was that being "me" was not an acceptable option.

While being able to adapt and modify behavior is one thing, it is not healthy to never feel that what you bring is enough. This carried on from childhood and with the deception of adultery, into my adult life. Part of the problem was that I did not know (ignorant) who I truly was. Hosea 4:6 says that God's people perish for lack of knowledge; because they have rejected knowledge. I wondered, how did I REJECT it? I now recognize that there were periods of time when I thought I was happy, but they were few and far between. It was not until I fully understood, gained the knowledge, and ACCEPTED that "I," yes "me," am ENOUGH that I have been able to move into real life and living. Unfortunately, I learned this late in life, but not too late!

Girlfriends were angry when I was given a compliment on my looks. Other mothers felt I had an advantage because my kids were relatively well-behaved. Coworkers felt I could not be sympathetic with their problems because I enjoyed a certain income level. I soon began to look for complaints in my life, although not consciously, in order to "fit in" and make others more comfortable with themselves. My pains and struggles were not visible, so people often felt they were cheated out of *MY* suffering!

I have plenty and enough pain to bare. I have enough love, enough joy, enough education, enough friends. I am smart enough, small enough, kind enough, strong enough, rich enough, and every other "enough" I need to move forward and complete this journey. I am no longer ignorant nor blind to what God has to say about me.

Psalms 139:14 says that I am fearfully and wonderfully made. Wow, I now know and accept His Word as Truth. I now acknowledge His voice and reject ignorance instead of thinking it's bliss. I am no longer blissfully ignorant nor knowingly blind. Instead, I choose to be joyful in knowing Me. Not who others want me to be, but who I am, and I am satisfied with me.

I thank God for taking me from ignorant bliss to knowledge and joy!

Ignorance, Bliss or Blindness

God doesn't leave you ignorant
He's given wisdom to you
If you follow his spirit
It will always guide you through

Things may now seem blissful
On the surface they may be
Blindness gives false perceptions
Of what you think you see

Knowledge, wisdom, and understanding
Are what we all should possess
If you choose them wisely
God will certainly handle the rest

Stay awoke with eyes wide open
Stay true to who you are
Wisdom can't reside with ignorance
Using wisdom will prevent life's scars

~Renita L. Smith

Reflections

_____

_____

_____

_____

_____

_____

_____

_____

_____

_____

_____

_____

_____

_____

_____

_____

_____

_____

_____

_____

When thinking about the times in life that have been the hardest to bear, it was often times of losing loved ones. Why did I have to lose the people who I care about the most? As a young adult, my kids were healthy and well behaved, and my spouse made a lot of money. On the surface, my life appeared to be wonderful, need I say *Perfect*! This was confirmed by the fact that people were always telling me how "lucky" or "blessed" I was. Some would even go as far as to get mad with me because of the apparent problems they were encountering. It was as if "I" did not deserve this life. So, why would I be sad or worried about anything. Everything that people normally worry about had been taken care of. The bills were paid. The children did their school work and participated in activities. I had a nice home and plenty of friends. Why on earth would I be concerned about what happens tomorrow?
Very few people, if any tried to go beneath the surface and to really get to know me.

They felt I had no reason or right to fear, pain or anxiety. After all, I had everything that anyone could ever ask for, right?

I believe that a lot of pain we experience is a byproduct of fear. Where did the pain or fear begin? I believe that both of these emotions became a part of me, gradually and over the most impressionable periods of my life. Every time there was a death or a divorce in the family, it was a lost and a cause for pain or fear. Let's begin by talking about death. While it did not appear to traumatize me as a child, I experienced the death of a lot of people who were especially close to me. I can remember my mother's aunt passing and I was about 4. She was sickened and would not get out of the bed for a couple of days. At around 5, I can remember going to a private school and the principal's daughter (I think she was one year older than me), was killed in an explosion at the store. I dreamed about her for a long time. I remember my best friend in the third grade, Dorothy. She lived across the street and we would walk to school together. I went to meet her one morning and she was ill. When school let out that afternoon, she passed. My step father went to his place of business one morning (I was about 11), and was murdered in his shop. I remember getting ready for a special weekend party with my long time on again off again friend from high school. We were in college now and this time it looked as if we might develop something special. I had planned to attend his 21st birthday party but received a call that my uncle had passed. My uncle was the same age as me and was more like a brother. I was devastated! My father was an only child. My mother didn't have any sisters, but she had 4 brothers. One of her brothers passed in 1980, 1981 and 1982. This was very traumatic.

Things seemed to settle down for a while, until my nephew was killed at the age of 17. Only one of the above deaths were somewhat expected. The others were very sudden. Some were very violent. The lesson life had taught was that people was here one day and gone the next. My mother passed of cancer and although her death was expected, I was still not prepared for the loss. My father did not play a major role in my life, but his passing was still something that I felt affected me. It seems strange to me when people say they have never lost anyone very close to them. I have lost both parents, close cousins, and several very special friends who were as close as family. I have to ask myself how these experiences have affected the way I look at life and how I react to it. I believe experiencing these losses, especially the sudden ones, have caused me to be more anxious and worried. I know that anxiety and worry directly contradicts God's words. I know that the Word says to be anxious for nothing and through prayer and supplication let your requests be known. What if my request is for no more pain? The answer is always in the Word. I had to ask why so many people that I love had to go.

The truth is that we all have an appointed time. Ecclesiastes 3 tells us that to everything there is a season. During times of heartbreak or pain, I have to remember that there will also be a time to sing and time to dance. I have to make the most of the moments that are pleasant.

There were instances when pain and fear brought me to my knees and I knew that there was no other help but in the Word.

When my spirit was broken, and I was afraid, it didn't matter what my external situation looked like. I believe that is why I have never been a person who is envious or jealous of someone else's situation. I had a close friend who was going through some painful experiences at the same time that I was. Our circumstances and experiences were different but, both our pain was just as profound as the other. Pain is pain. You never know what a person is experiencing internally. When cheating occurs and a person is consistently assured in the relationship that they are imagining changed behavior or wrongfully accusing an innocent person, they begin to question their own thoughts.

Once someone gets you to question yourself, they can easily start to diminish your self-esteem. People don't usually recognize the hurt, the internal bleeding and the emotional brutality involved in adulterous affairs. If someone is robbed at gunpoint, shot and left bleeding, everyone is sympathetic and no one blames the victim. When your heart is "ripped out" and the knife is left and twisted in your flesh after adultery, some will even say to you that it's your fault. It's as if society accepts the brutality of the act, as long as no one has to *see* the blood. While the analogy may be exaggerated, it clearly represents the message. Certainly, the extent of the pain one experiences and the timing of circumstances, all play a major role in our responses. All of our support systems are also key in helping us to "handle" our circumstances, whatever they may be. Walking in fear is not of God. I literally had gotten to the point where I was always on edge about who would die next and careful not to fully trust people anymore. Losing loved ones did however, teach me to always treat others with kindness. I realize that I really do not know when it will be my last time to see them. Death is a permanent release of pain and sickness for the deceased. On the other hand, sometimes painful lessons may simply be a reminder to appreciate others and to not take them for granted. Pain can remind you that YOU are human, it can also bring you back to God.

I have discovered that the love of God really does cast out all fear. I know I cannot walk in faith and walk in fear simultaneously. I have to make a daily decision and I have to choose for love to prevail. I have to choose to walk in faith, knowing that God WILL NOT place more on me (or my family) than I can bear. Even when it *feels* unbearable. I choose to accept God's plan.

I thank God for His faithfulness and for His strength in times of sorrow

Pain

Why so much pain
Lingering in my soul
Must I endure
Trying to reach my goal

Struggling every day
Trying to make it in
Loss of many loved ones
Spouse, family, and friends

Why so much pain
In this world I know
Broken and afraid
Not knowing where to go

How do I go on
While living with this pain
I just trust in Jesus
His love it shall remain

~Renita L. Smith

Reflections

Question #4 Why Am I Being Rejected?

Wow, I had only been in my new city for 20 months and found myself packing yet again. Previously, I stayed in another city for 14 months.   I moved to another state where I didn't know anyone and to a city that I had never visited. I quickly began to fit in and to learn my way around. I even started what I thought would be a major lifestyle change.   I was doing great while working with a trainer, then I had to have emergency surgery because of an abscess in my abdomen. I was determined not to be deterred. I started a walking regiment as soon as I could, but then I had to have surgery on my knee. I concluded that God must be rejecting my efforts to lose the weight because all my enthusiasm and attempts to get fit were blocked by the surgeries. To add insult to injury, I did not find the compassion during my illnesses that I felt should have come from "certain" of my new co-workers.   I literally went to work with a 4x5cm hole in my abdomen! I was grateful for those who showed compassion, brought me food and the kindness of the students who felt it a privilege to wheel me around the building.

It's funny how we often look to the wrong people for friendship and compassion. There were some ladies who were members of a line dance group that volunteered to be my "family." Despite the kindness and caring of so many people, I quickly retreated into my private world, noting the attitudes of the few.

After the two unexpected surgeries and prompting from my son, I decided to relocate back to Texas. But, my disappointment with certain people have always played a part of my nomadic behavioral. Initially, feeling rejected and wanting a fresh start had played a major role in my decision to move away from my home town. I moved back home when I felt enough time had passed and I would be welcomed again. Once home, I decided there was still too much unacceptance and back stabbing. I found myself constantly being reminded of people who had betrayed me. One of my former "good friends" refused to speak to me at a fundraising event, but wanted to give me a hug when I visited her church.

 It really didn't matter how insignificant these people were in my life, I gave more focus to them than to the ones who welcomed me and offered me a place to belong. Despite my tough exterior, I guess I expected and didn't understand when people were not accepting of me. Please note the statement is in the *past tense*!

No one was ever harder on me than I have always been on myself. Whenever anyone engaged me into conflict, I would become impassioned and enraged because I wanted to be understood. Rejection had somehow become my kryptonite because I felt if anyone knows me, they should accept me. They had to understand my heart.
But when I think about Jesus, I often think about how He was rejected and betrayed by someone who had walked with Him for so long. They knew HIS heart! How painful.

How did He handle rejection? I know I am not Christ, but I am certainly striving to be more like Him. He kept the course when he was rejected, knowing there was more hurt and anguish to come.

I am a person who will stand up for herself and because of this, people often misread me and think I am a person who is ready to engage in conflict. Truth be told, when it comes to fight or flight, I would choose to "fly away" if given the opportunity. This does not mean that I will not stand up for myself or my loved ones. This is where so many people become disillusioned. We often want to be seen in one light but are misunderstood because of the vantage point that we present.

Yes, God knows the heart, but men only know what we present to them. I have learned that if I want to be seen for who I am, I have to learn to show more of what's inside. We like to say that God is "on the inside," but doesn't allow Him to show up on the outside. We most often show ourselves through our conversations. The way we talk. James 3:13 refers to a wise man as one who shows meekness of wisdom through his "good conversation." I had to examine how to have "meekness" in my conversations. This is something I am definitely still working on. But, working I am!! My conversations are typically not bad or malicious, but I find myself trying to defend or to prove myself. I try to speak for the underdog and hate malicious gossip.

I have had to learn how to communicate my thoughts with confidence while not appearing confrontational. Although some people will reject me for no reason at all, I want to be certain that I do not do or say anything that justifies their behavior. The Word says to never let your good be spoken evil of. When I feel someone has wronged me or spoke unkindly of me, I so often wanted to "put them in check." I have had a reputation for being outspoken at any cost. Reality is that even if you prove a point or correct an error, some people will reject you *because* you are right.

Exodus 14:14 says that the Lord will fight for you and you should hold your peace. I have had to learn that I should just let some things go. Those times when I feel I need to speak up and know that what I have to say will not change the situation or perception, I am making the choice not to speak. I have learned that I must allow God to lead me into not only what to say, but also when to say it. I must allow His spirit rather than my passion to lead. Then and only then will I be able to withstand the rejection and misunderstandings that are sure to come. The lesson has been that being like God means being meek and lowly. That doesn't make me weak and low!

Thank you, Lord for your Word, and creating me Wonderfully

Rejected

Why am I often rejected
When all I want is to be free
Free to live in service
To those who engage me

Friends show no compassion
When I am going through
So, I chose to run away
To find a life anew

Why am I often rejected
By those I hold so dear
Feeling they will comfort me
Yet abandoned and brought to tears

People chose to reject me
For no reason at all
So, I keep it moving
Continuing to stand tall

I tried to live in their world
I needed to fit in
Once again rejection showed up
I retreated to my world within

Then I thought about Jesus
Rejected I may be
He kept the course while being rejected
So, I can live and be free

He paid the ultimate price
This I know is true
No more fear of rejection
For me or for you

~Renita L. Smith

Reflections

Question #5   How Do I Live Free?

It's funny how we all have those places in our lives that have held us captive. Sometimes we are prisoners of our own minds and circumstances. For some of us it's a place, a building or a city. Some are held by drug, alcohol or gambling addictions. Pride, self-loathing and low self-esteem are some of the most ruthless captors. A person's friends, parents or even children can be holding cells with double locks or lost keys. In Jeremiah 29, the prophet sent a letter to the people of Jerusalem who had been held captive in Babylon. He informed them that the Lord had thoughts of peace, not evil to give them and an "expected" end. Jeremiah continuously employed the people to seek peace and to not fall to false prophets and negative speakers.

Why is it so hard for me to believe the "Good News" and yet never struggle to believe the lies that Satan sends to imprison my mind? My captivity has come in the form of my acceptance of negative communication and the rehashing of bad or unfavorable memories.

I recently thought of so many wrong choices I made when it came to listening to friends throughout the years. I allowed so many people to put me down because it always seemed to make them feel as if they were ok with themselves. "Best" friends who would call to invite me to go somewhere only after others had declined or could not make it. I remember preparing for my wedding and sharing my list of the bridal party with my "bestie" at the time. She told me that the women I had chosen were thin and therefore, no one would be looking at me. She said I needed to lose a whole other person to stand next to them.... wow! I remember in school deciding to run for a particular office and my then "bestie" said I shouldn't because I was sure to lose. Others encouraged me to run, but I backed out because of my friend's opinion. I don't remember getting enough positive feedback from those who I allowed to feed into my spirit on a regular basis. No wonder I became so insecure and self-conscious.

As far back as I can remember, I have always been the person who would befriend a wide array of people. I accepted others into my life without examining their purpose or their motives. I've even allowed people in my home whom could now be classified as "no more than an enemy!" If I had any, LOL! Even when I started exercising and watching my weight, I was told I was being selfish and self-centered. I absorbed so much negativity and emotional garbage that I became toxic to myself. "Lord, how can I live free of all these things I've internalized that have given me a captive mindset?"

In searching the scriptures for an answer, I came upon Jeremiah. Jeremiah 29:12-13 tells me that I have to pray unto the Lord. But not just pray, I have to seek and search for Him with all my heart. I wondered why this passage is so redundant. The words seek, and search are obviously synonymous. Aren't they? I now understand what to seek and search means. I remember when I used to ask my sons to help me to find something. They would usually look on top of the surfaces. But, if the need to find the lost item was urgent enough, they would search (look harder) underneath everything! If the lost object was important, I would remind them to remove the chair cushions and lift anything placed in the way. We would even sometimes move the furniture around.

I have finally recognized that when God says to seek and to search, I have to not just read the scripture and look at what it says. I have to remove all the fear and the doubt. I have to lift the good memories and to remove the ones that were not pleasant. I must push the pain out of the way and rise up to study His word. I may even have to move some people (no matter how well intended they are), out of my way.

Finally, in the 14th verse of Jeremiah, it says that the Lord will turn away my captivity. This gives me consolation in that even if my captivity resides in my own mind, he can renew my thoughts and give me freedom.

I now know that my job is to seek Him, and He Will do the rest. I don't have to fight any addictions (including food), friends (when unsupportive), family (when misunderstood), or any other spiritual foe that I may encounter.

He will bring me to that same place and I can be at peace, bold and most of all enjoy my freedom despite the things that have so easily beset me. Whom the Lord set free is truly free indeed!

Thank you Lord for giving me knowledge of your word and the wisdom to seek understanding

How Do I Live Free?

How do I live free
From images in my mind
Strive only to please God
Then peace my soul shall find

Where do I find peace
In a world so filled with hate
Find my secret place
On bended knees I pray

Who can give me joy
When pain is all around
Stay grounded in my faith
To be on solid ground

What am I to do
To escape captivity
Enslavement of my mind
Unable to just be free

When will I overcome
The perils that I face
Only when I let go
Let God control my fate

How do I live free
Free to just be me
Put my trust in God
To lead me to my destiny   *~Renita L. Smith*

Reflections

I could have written about domestic violence, attempted rape, attempted suicide or even attempted murder. While those topics might intrigue and stimulate some more than the incidents mentioned, they would not have served the purpose for this particular piece of written work. I once gave someone gifts as a sincere act of kindness and was later told they felt I was just trying to make them like me. This book is about recognizing that when people are not kind or generous, they cannot easily accept kindness or generosity from others. When people do not feel good about themselves, they do not acknowledge what it good about those around them. My purpose is to bring to the forefront that most negativity is not about the person who receives it, but the source from which it originates.

I have often heard that to change one habit, you must replace it with another. This book is about my decision keep the positive and to discord the negative. This book is about closure. I remember my brother telling some neighborhood kids how smart I was. I was about 4 or 5 and he was really proud of how well I read. What a compliment!

Yes, those are the memories and events that I choose to keep close to my heart and mind. I have moved to 4 different cities in the past 5 years. Every place I went, I was met by wonderful people with positive attitudes and positive interactions. These are the people and the things I choose to allow to penetrate my soul.

In the end, it does not matter how others see you as much as how you see yourself. With that said, you must be careful of the lens in which you choose as your reflection instrument. You cannot continuously ingest poison and not eventually get sick, OR DIE! Why did they kill me? Because I allowed it and sometimes even invited them home! Instead of looking at myself in the eyes of others, I look in the mirror everyday and humbly tell myself how pleased I am with the person I have become. I remind myself of how much I appreciate my loving and kind heart, and how beautiful I am. The best part about it is that I know it all to be true! The purpose of this writing is that hopefully some others will recognize themselves in something I've shared and make a decision to see themselves as God has said.

www.ingramcontent.com/pod-product-compliance
Lightning Source LLC
Chambersburg PA
CBHW031226090426
42740CB00007B/729